The Splendor of Footbridges

An Emma Rose Sparrow Book

Copyright © 2015 Emma Rose Sparrow
All rights reserved.
Publish Date: November 14, 2015

Editor-in-Chief: Connor Chagnon
Sterling Elle Publishing
Bradford, Massachusetts

ISBN-13: 978-1519314529
ISBN-10: 1519314523

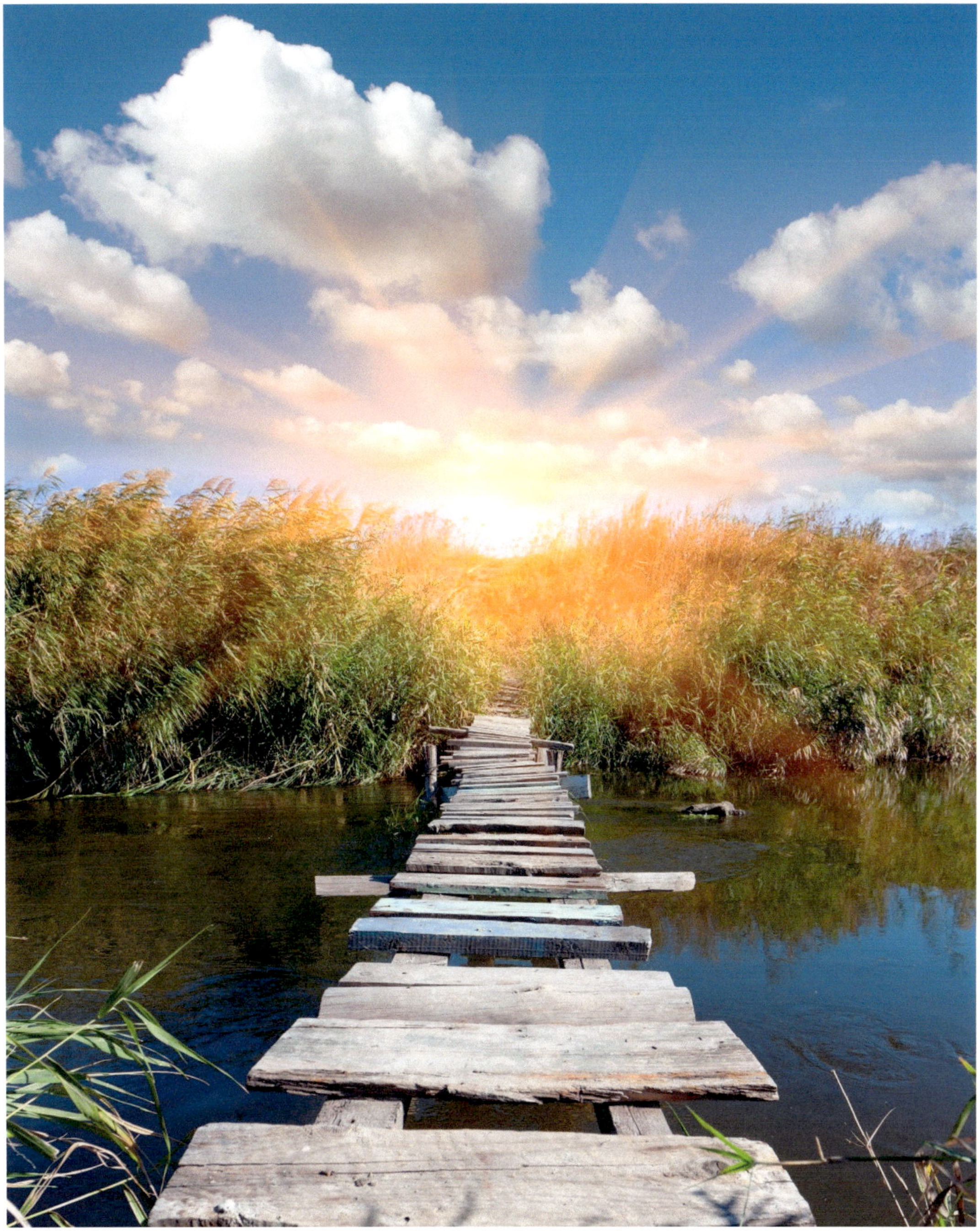

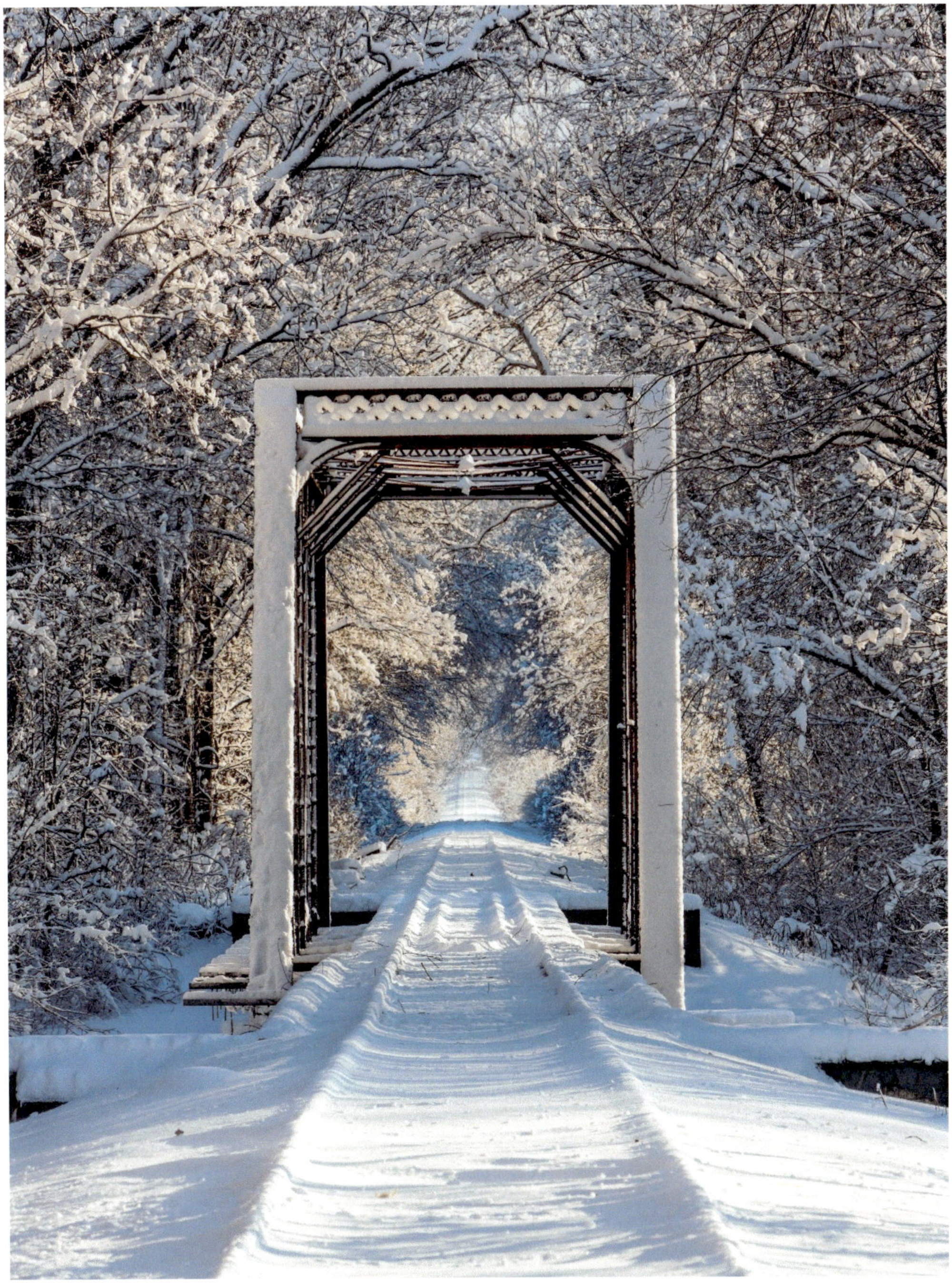

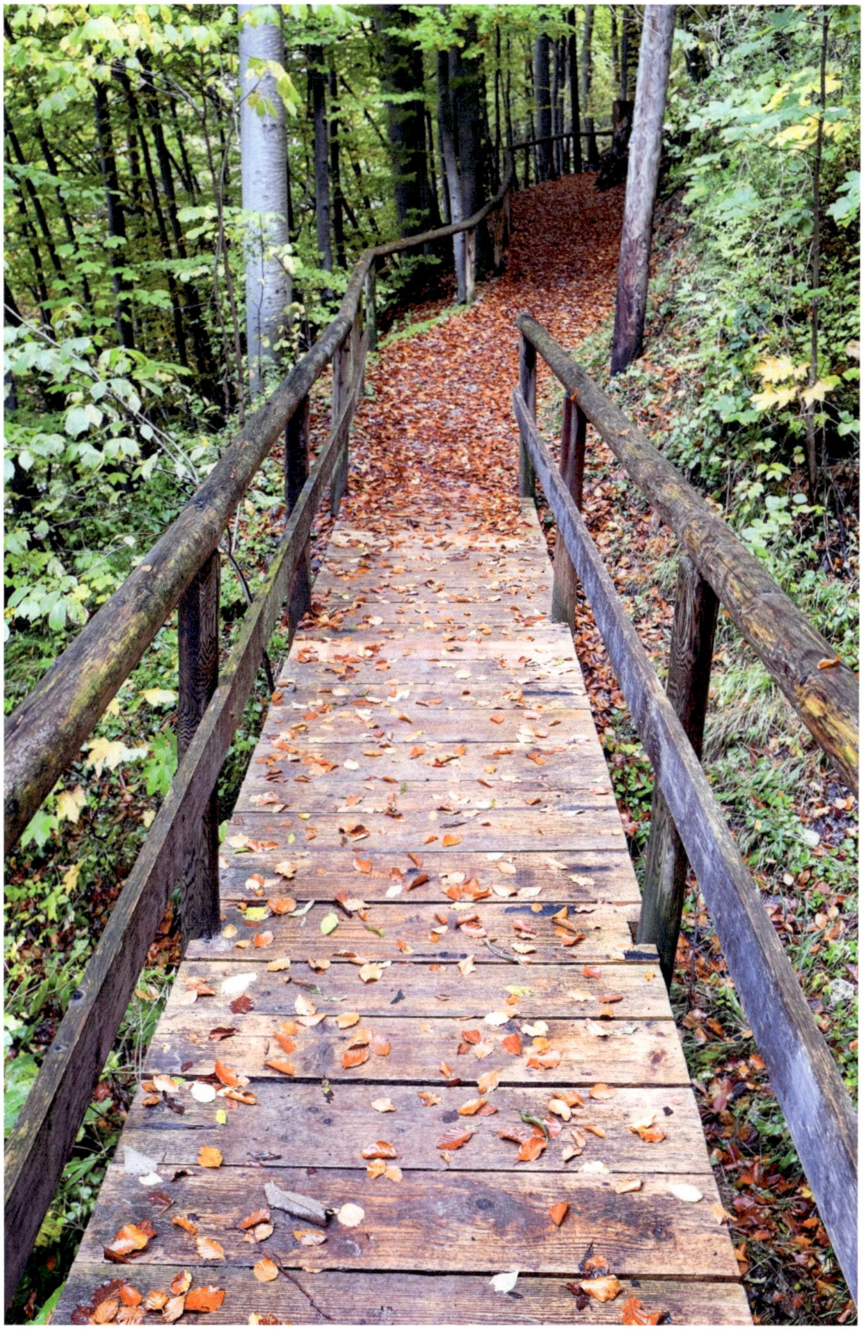

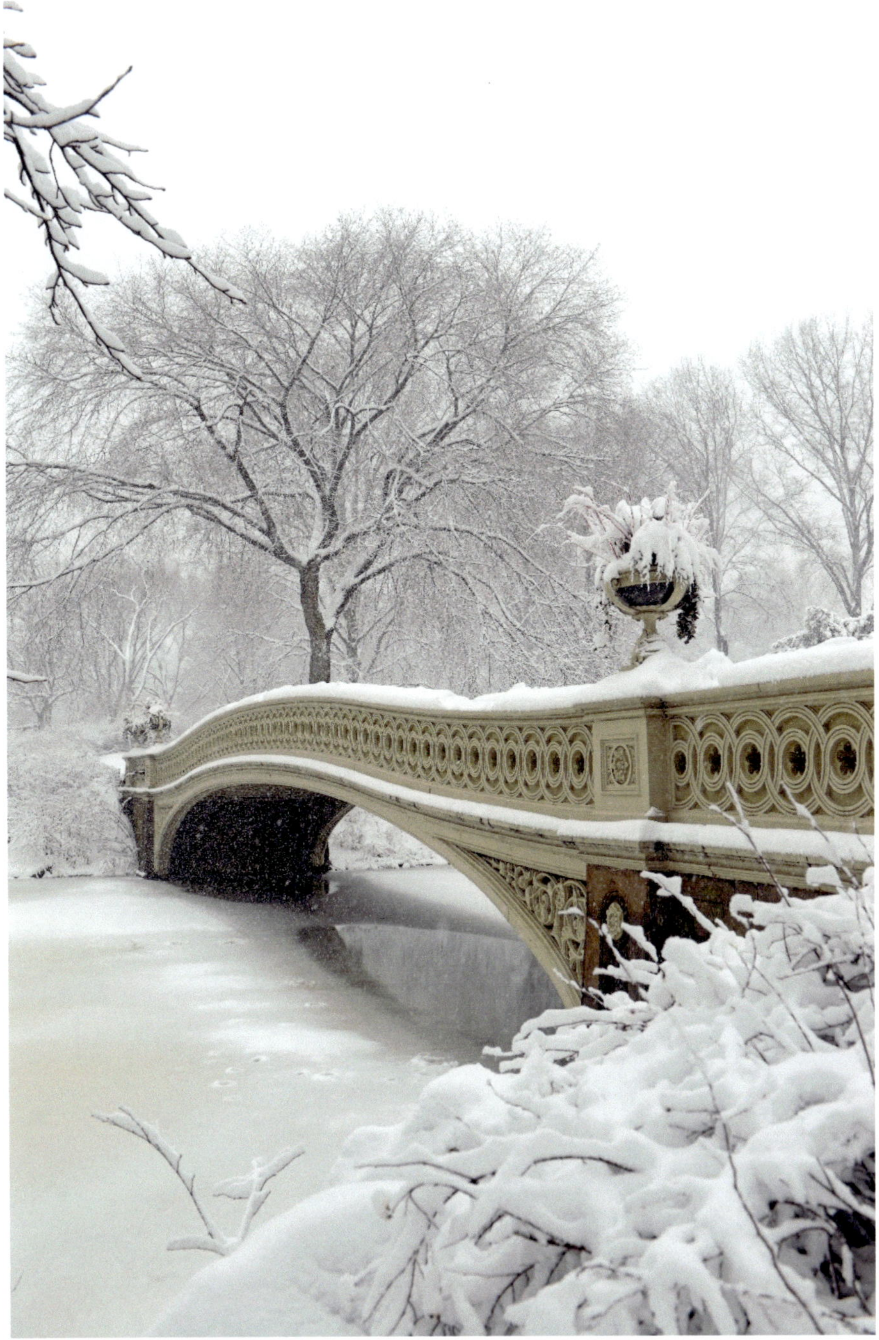

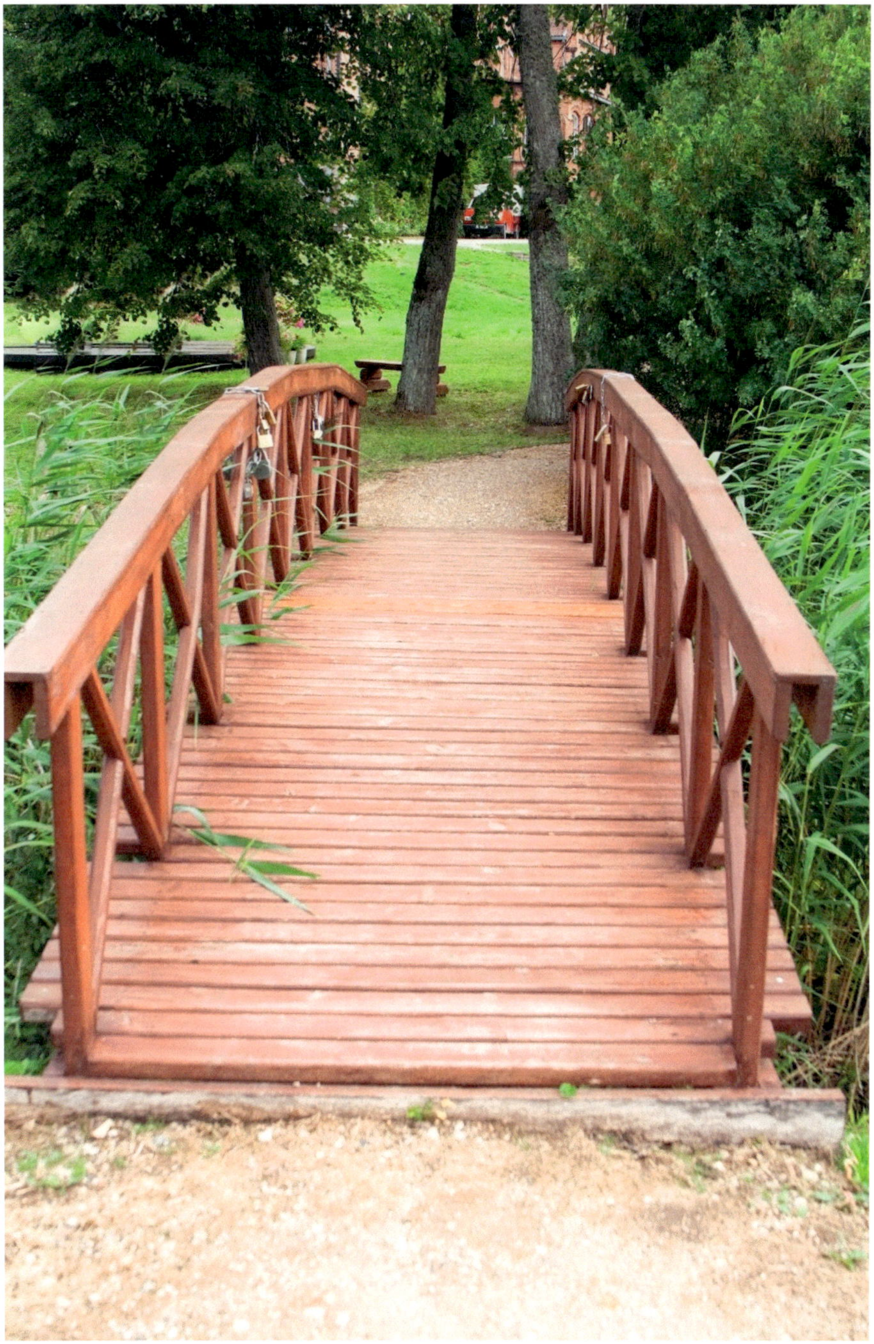

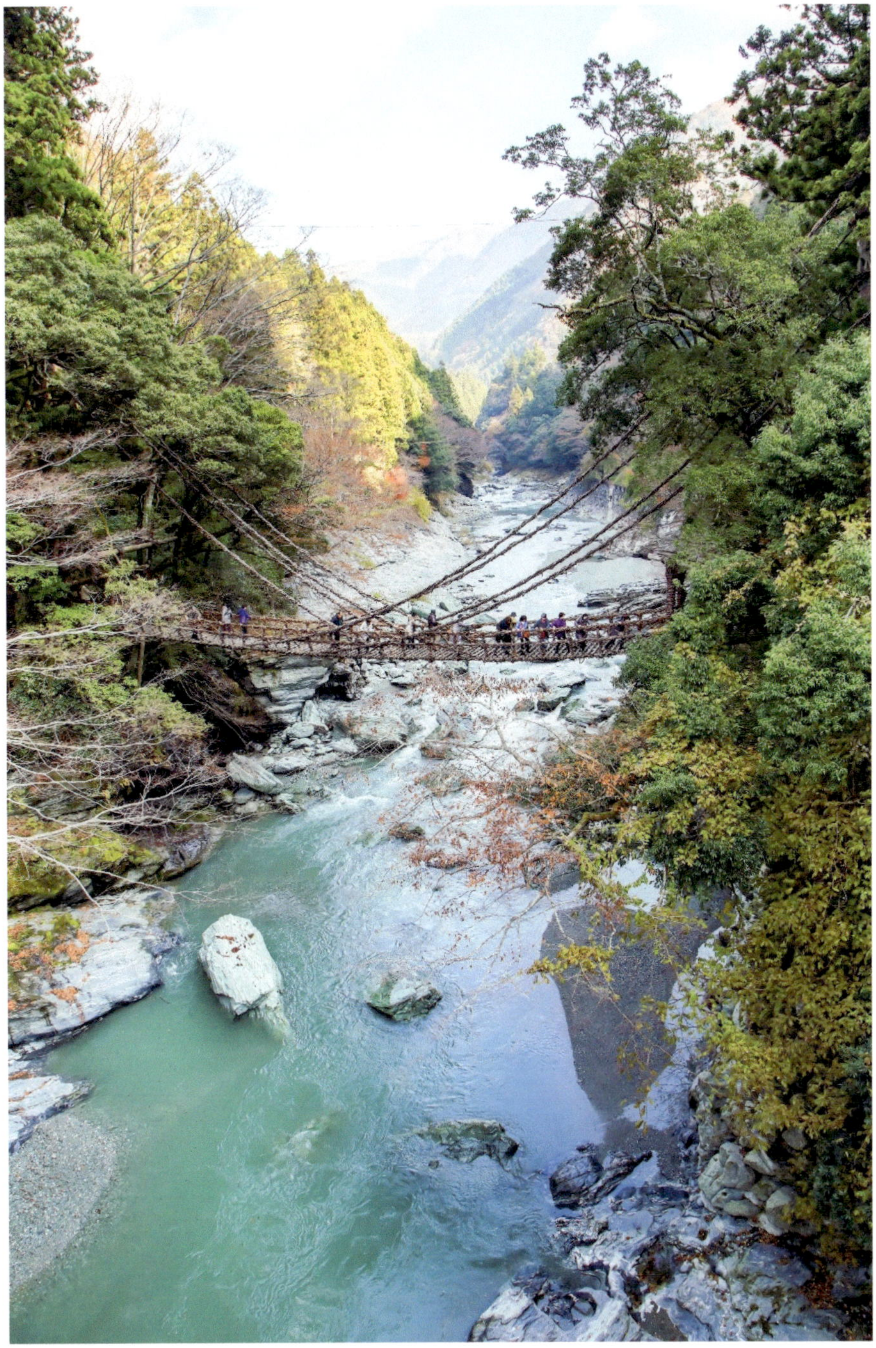

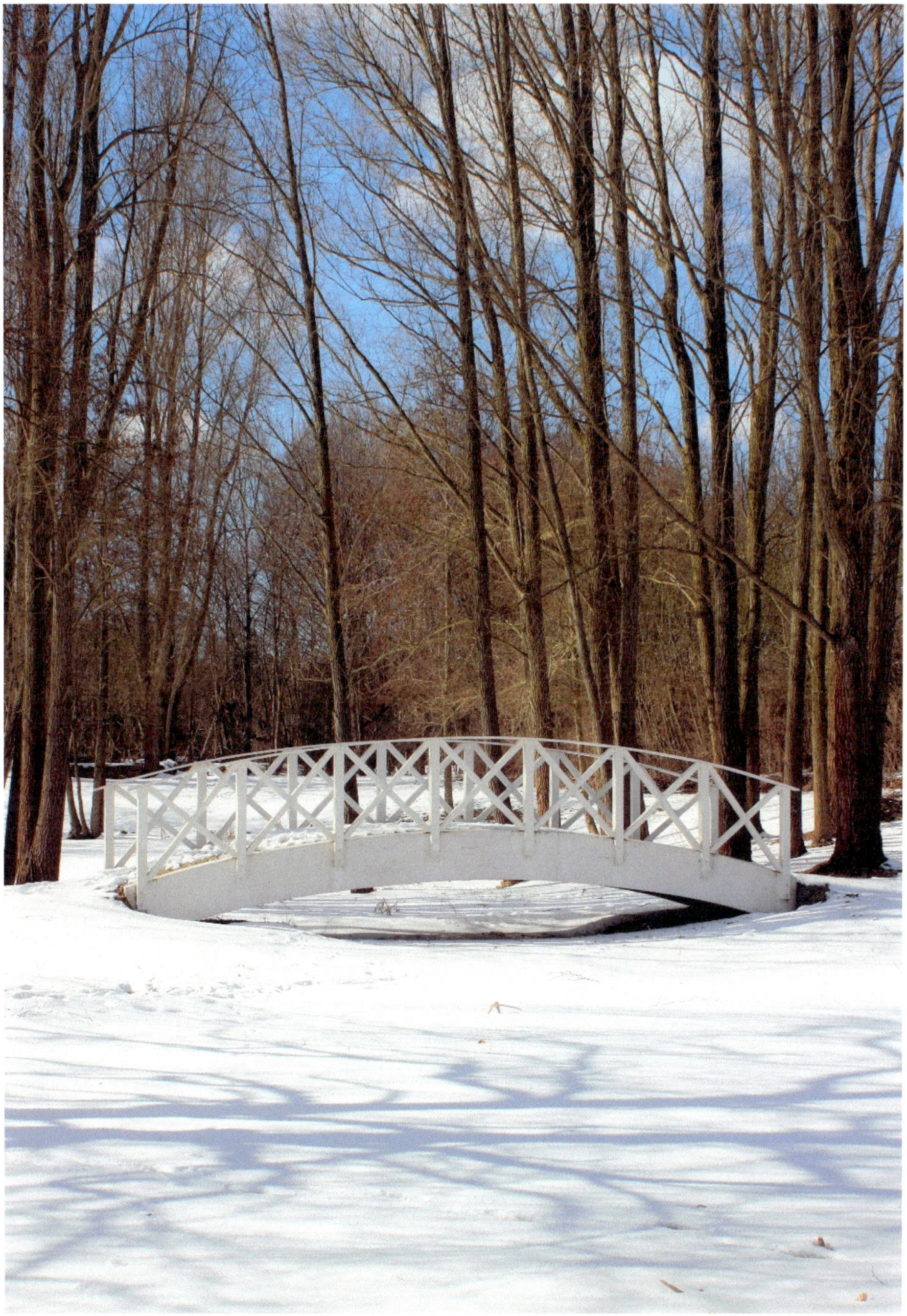

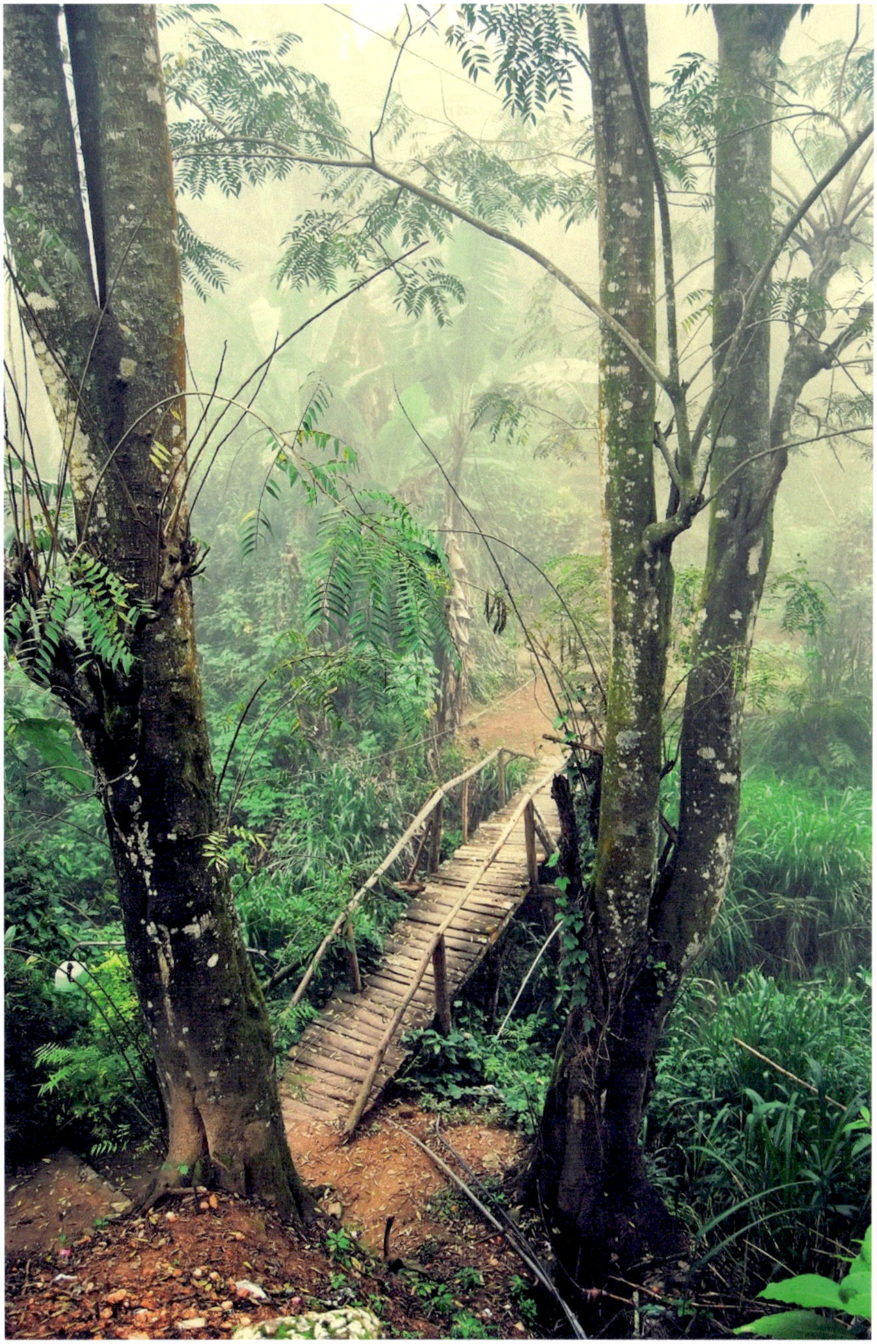

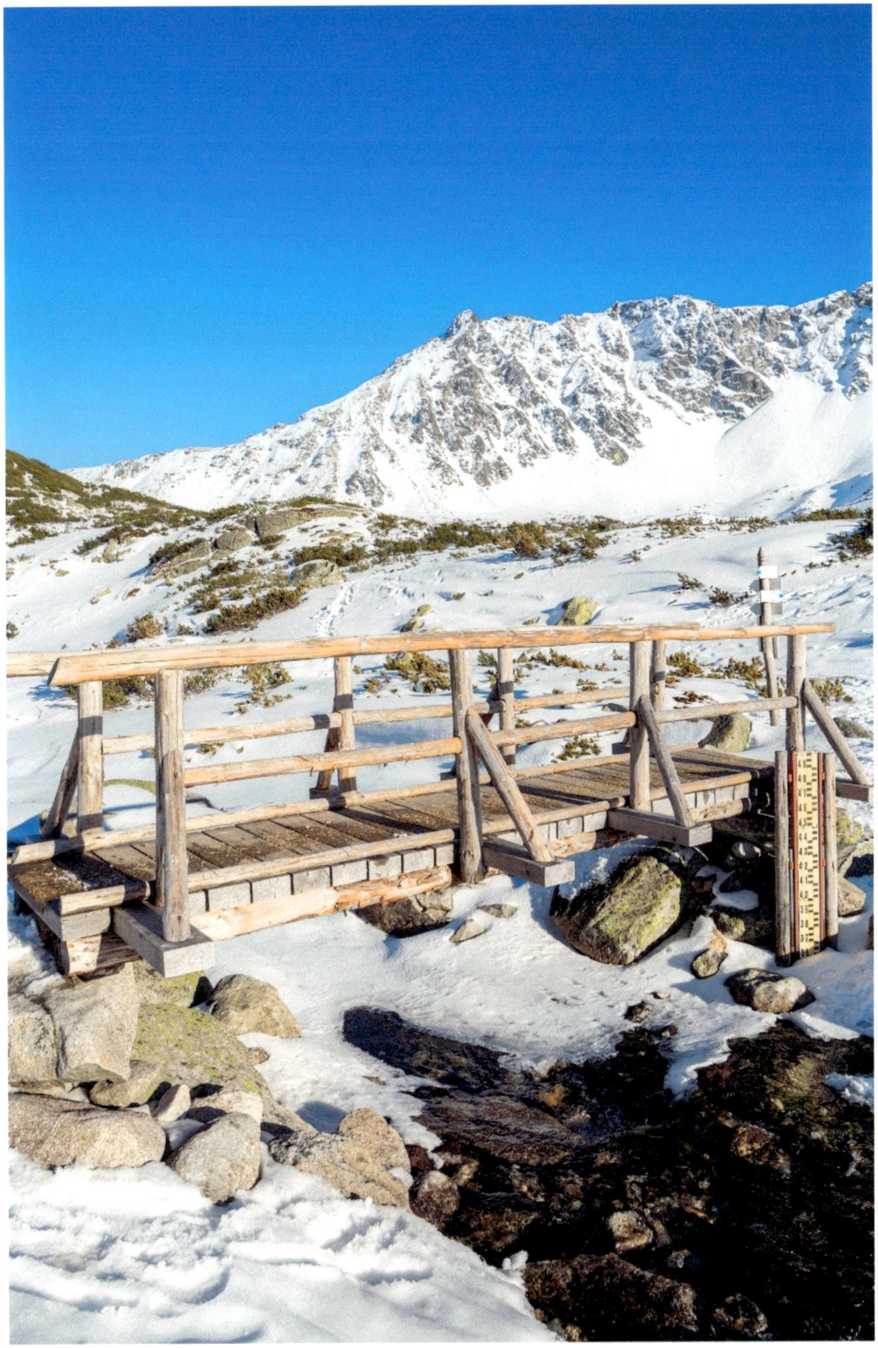

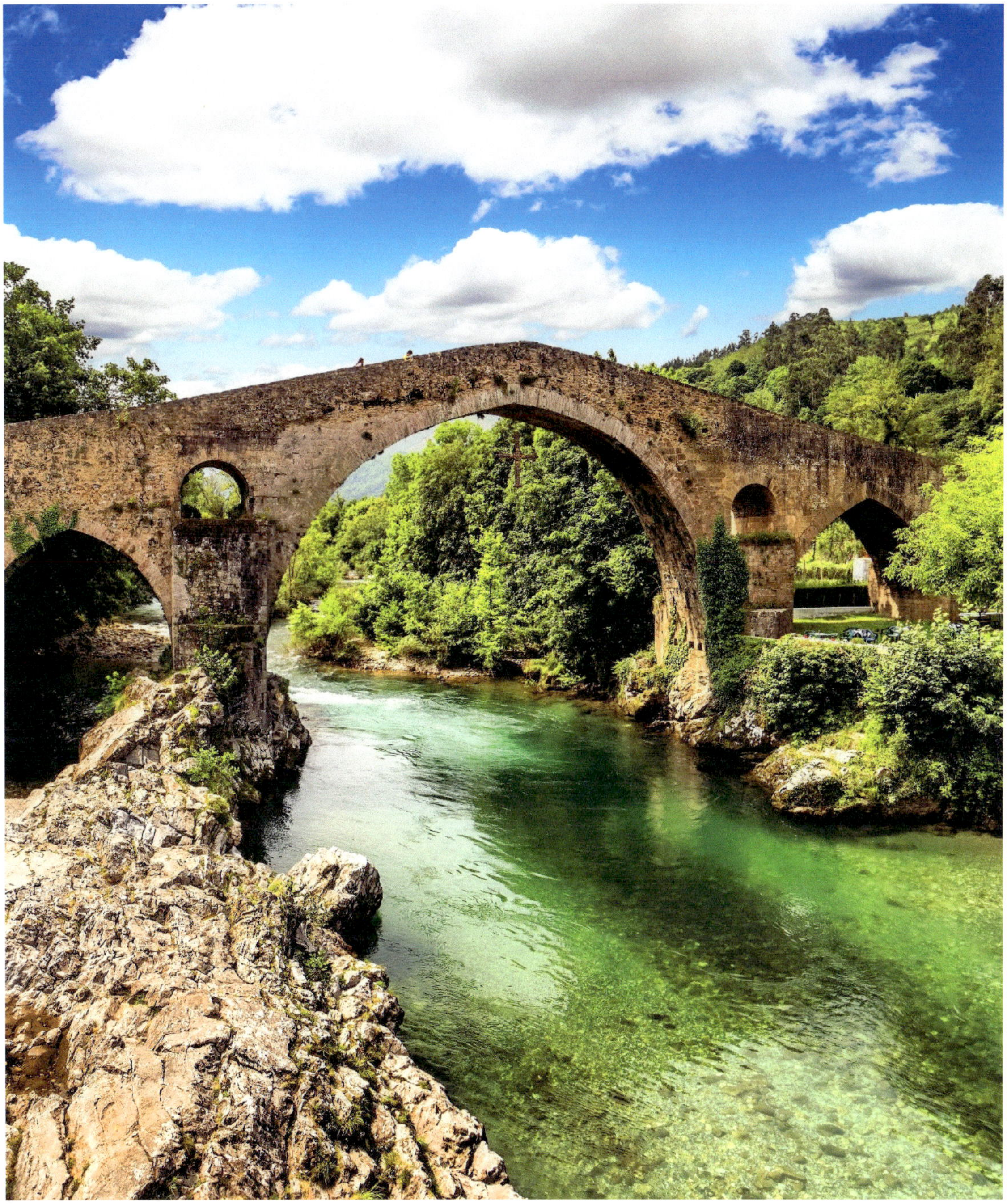

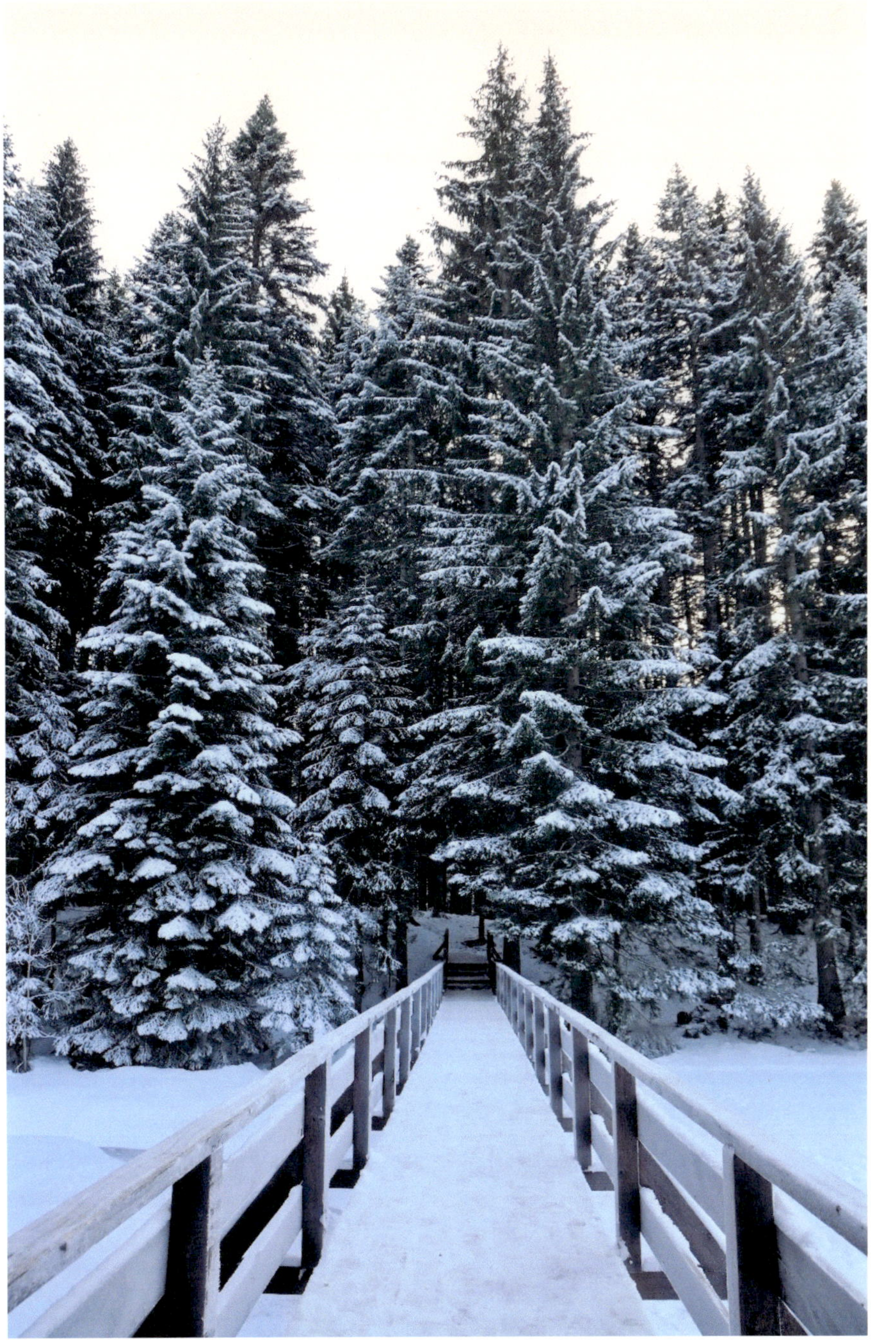

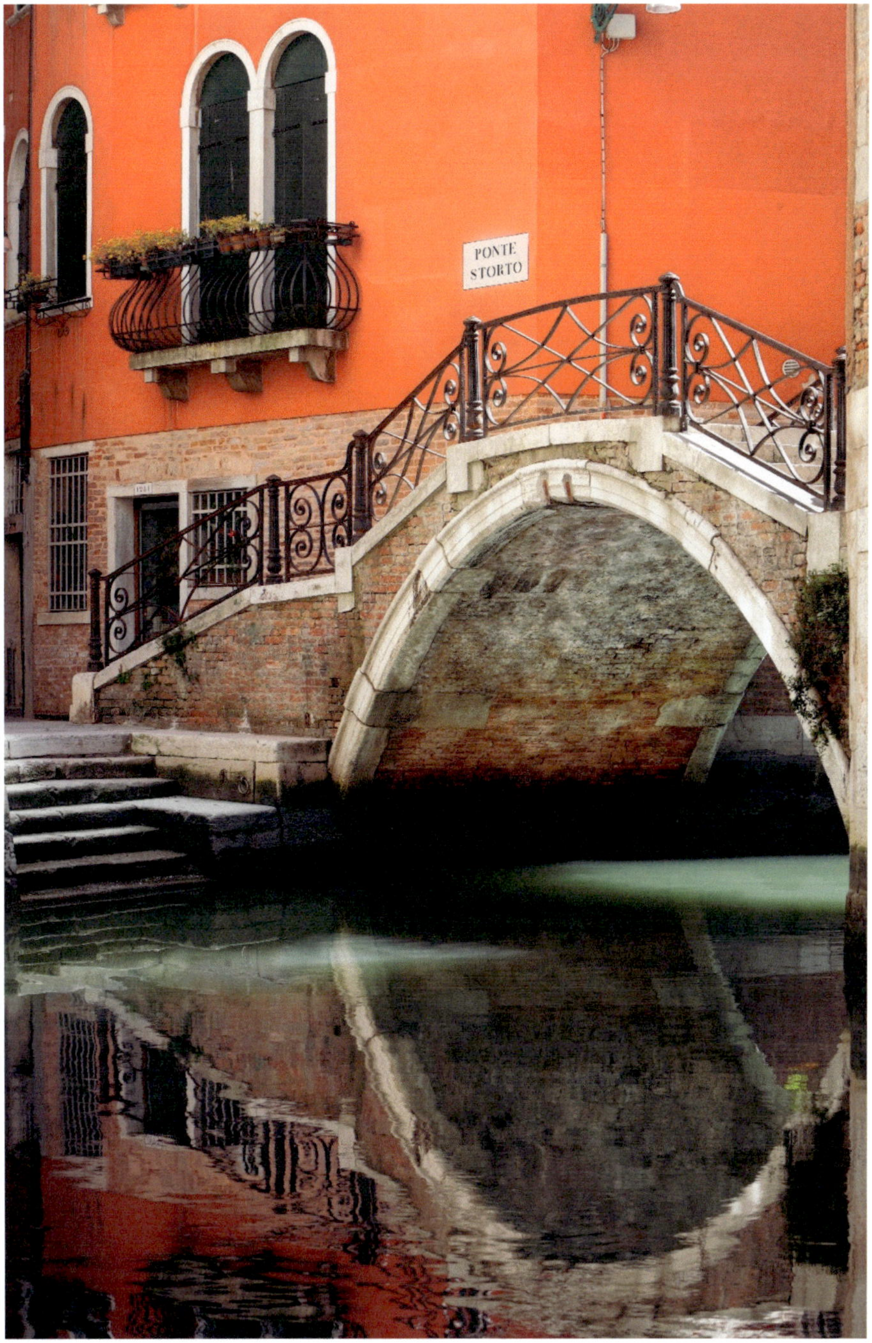
PONTE
STORTO

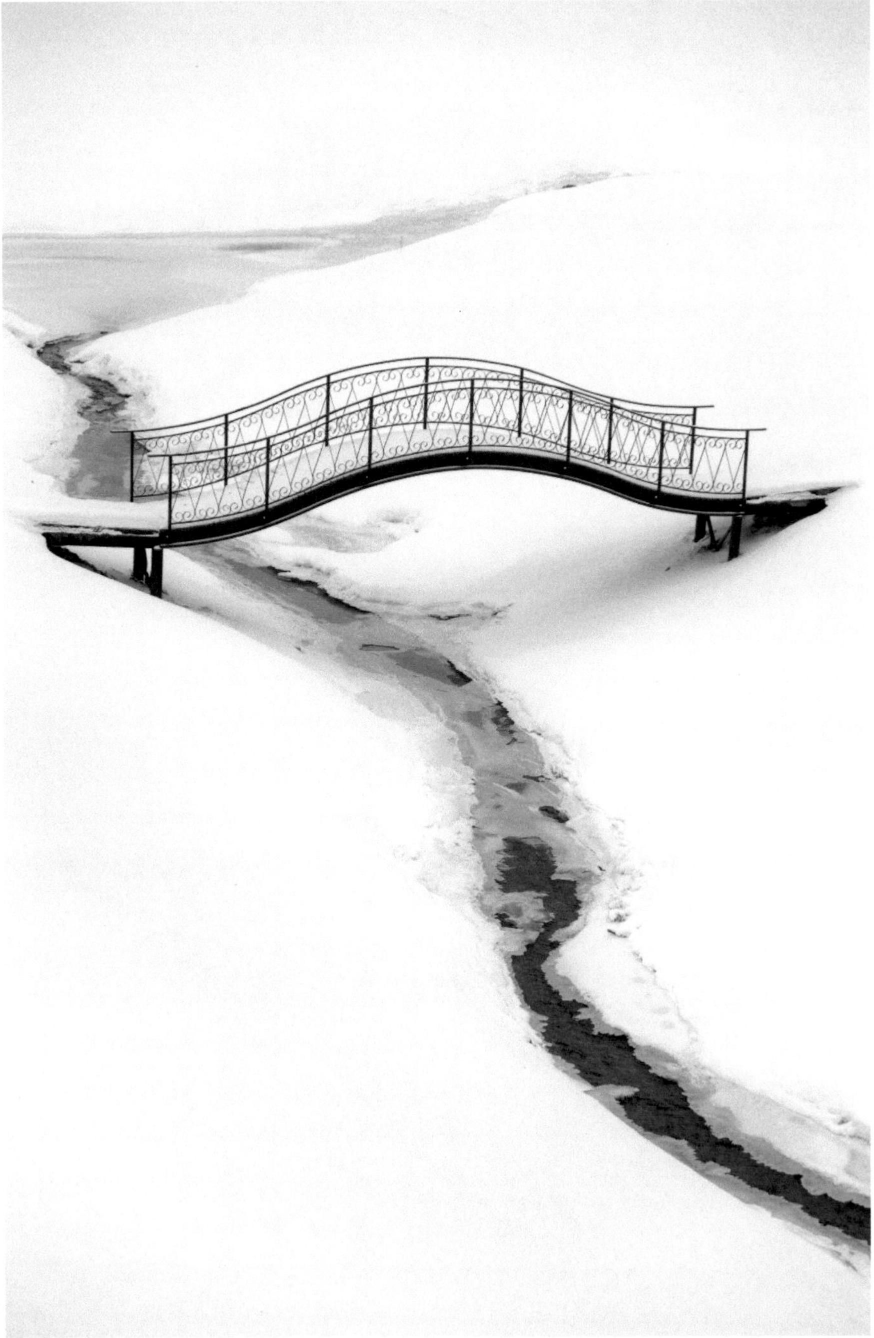

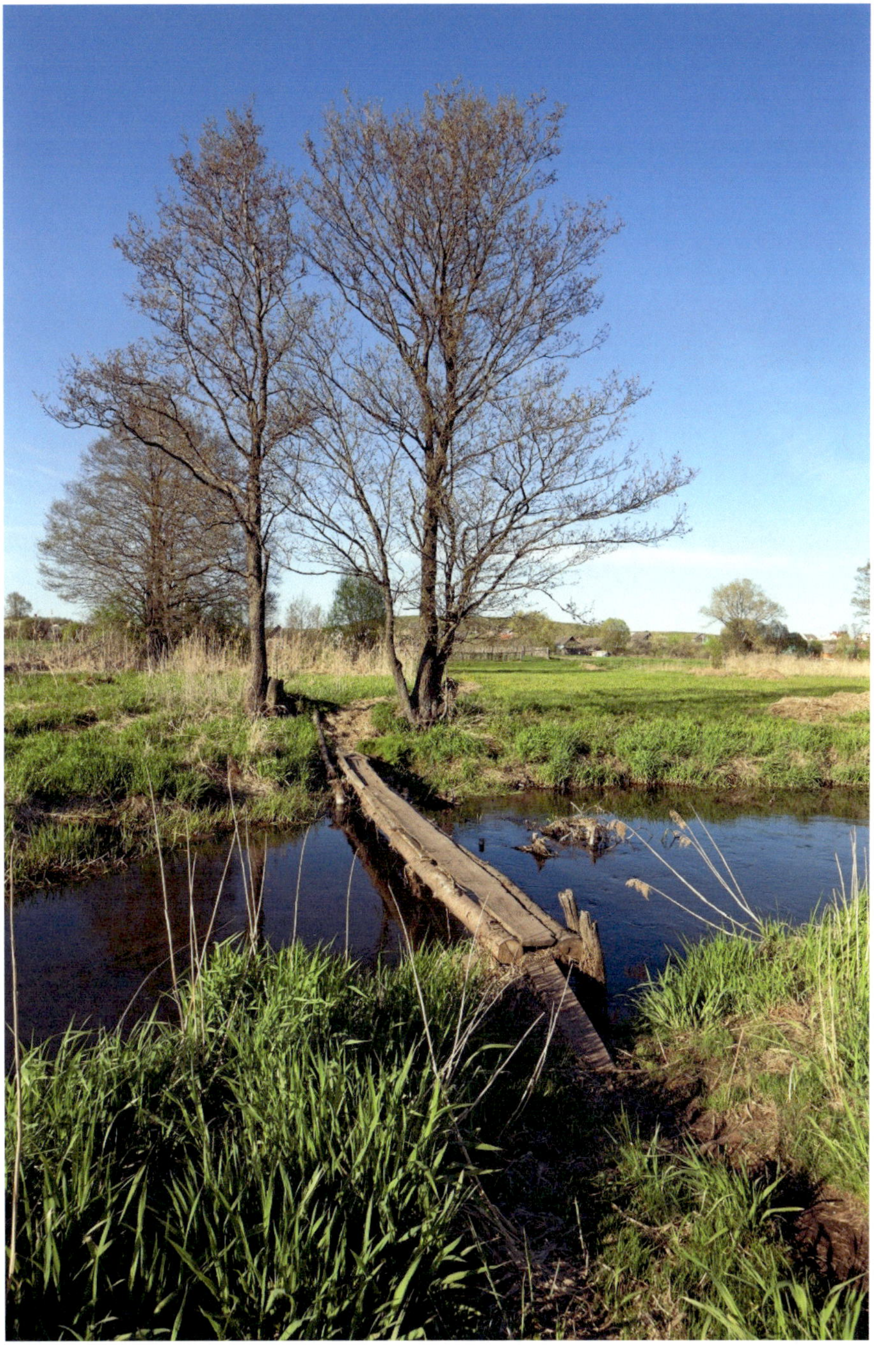

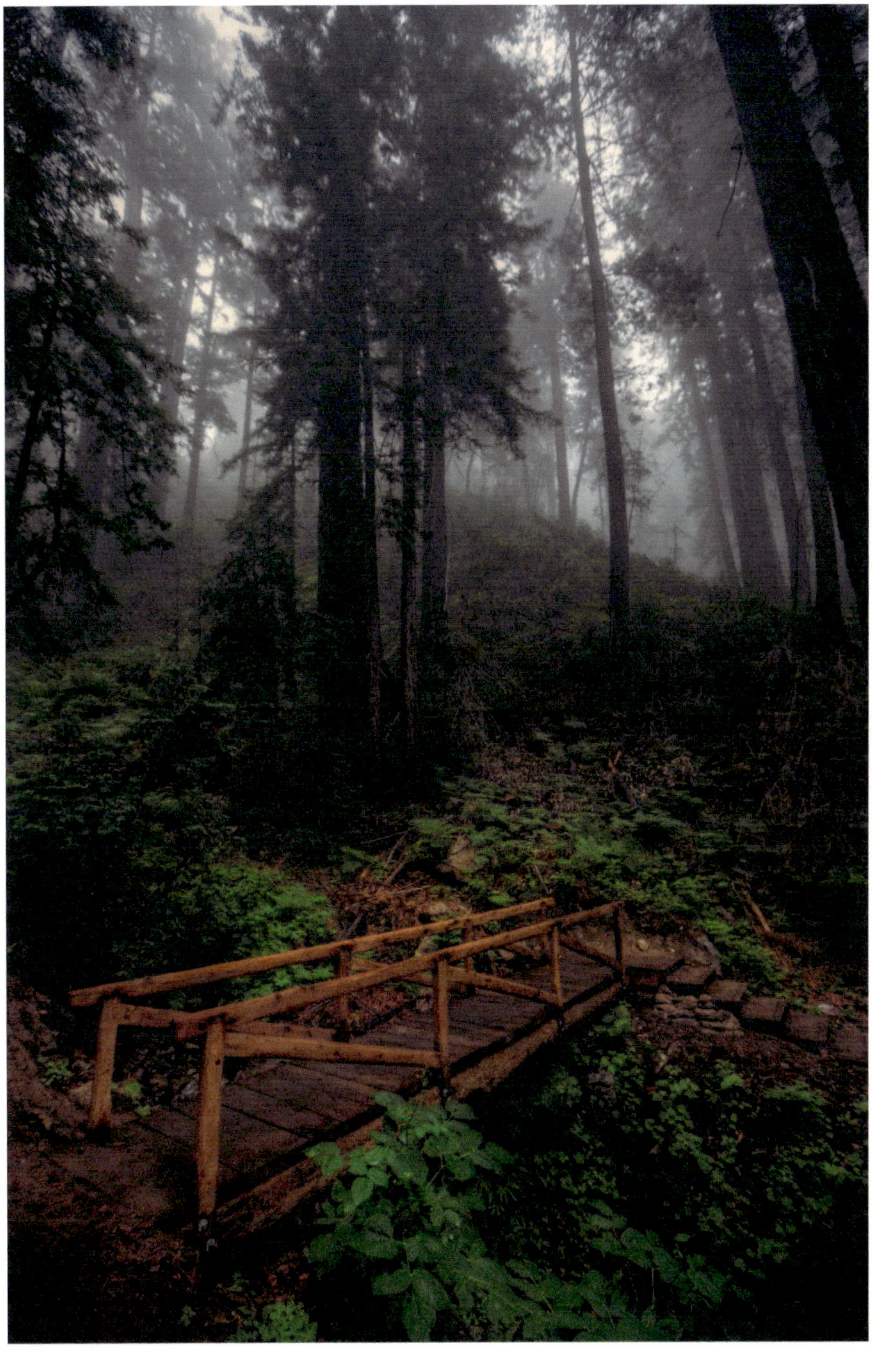

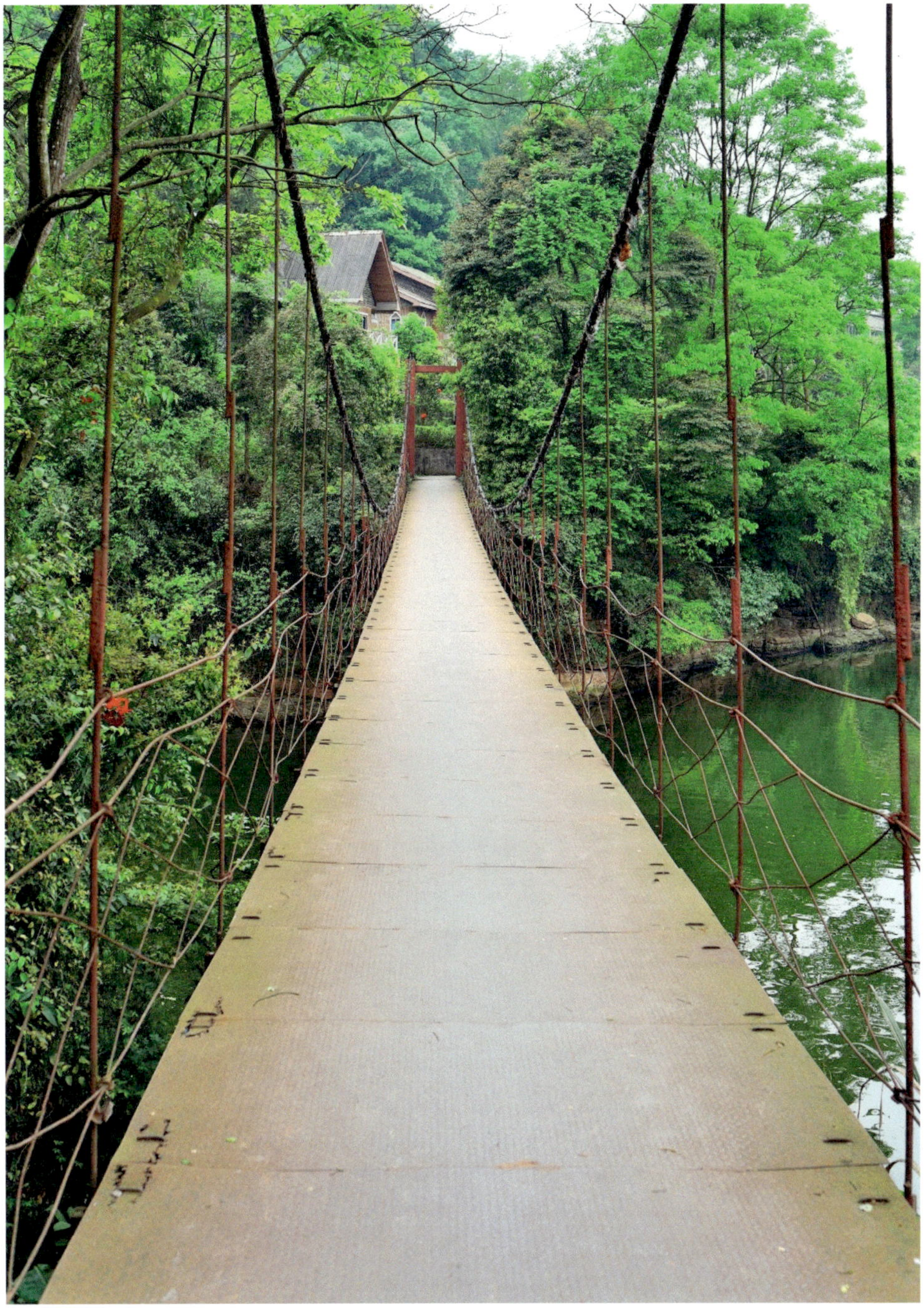

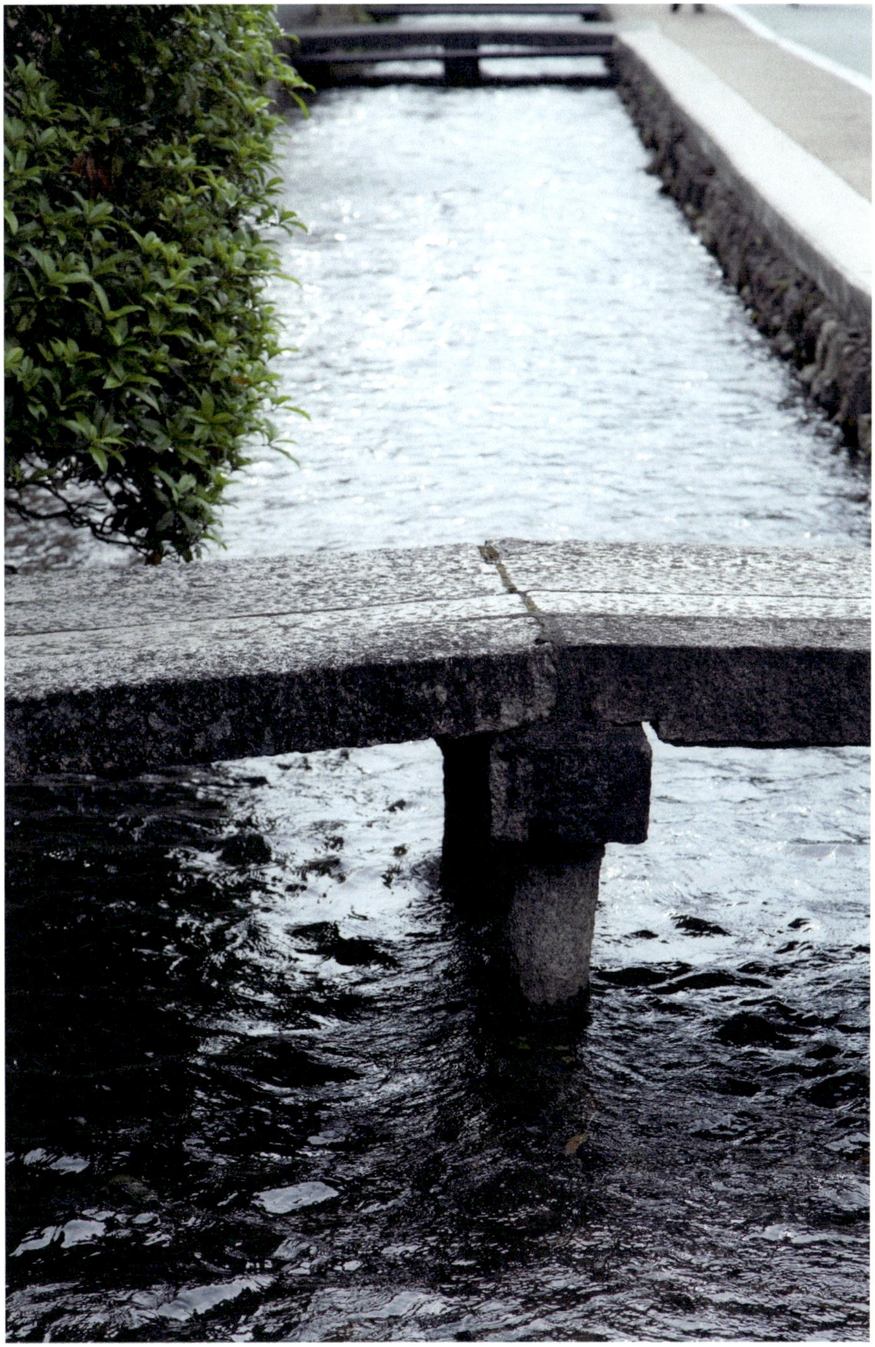

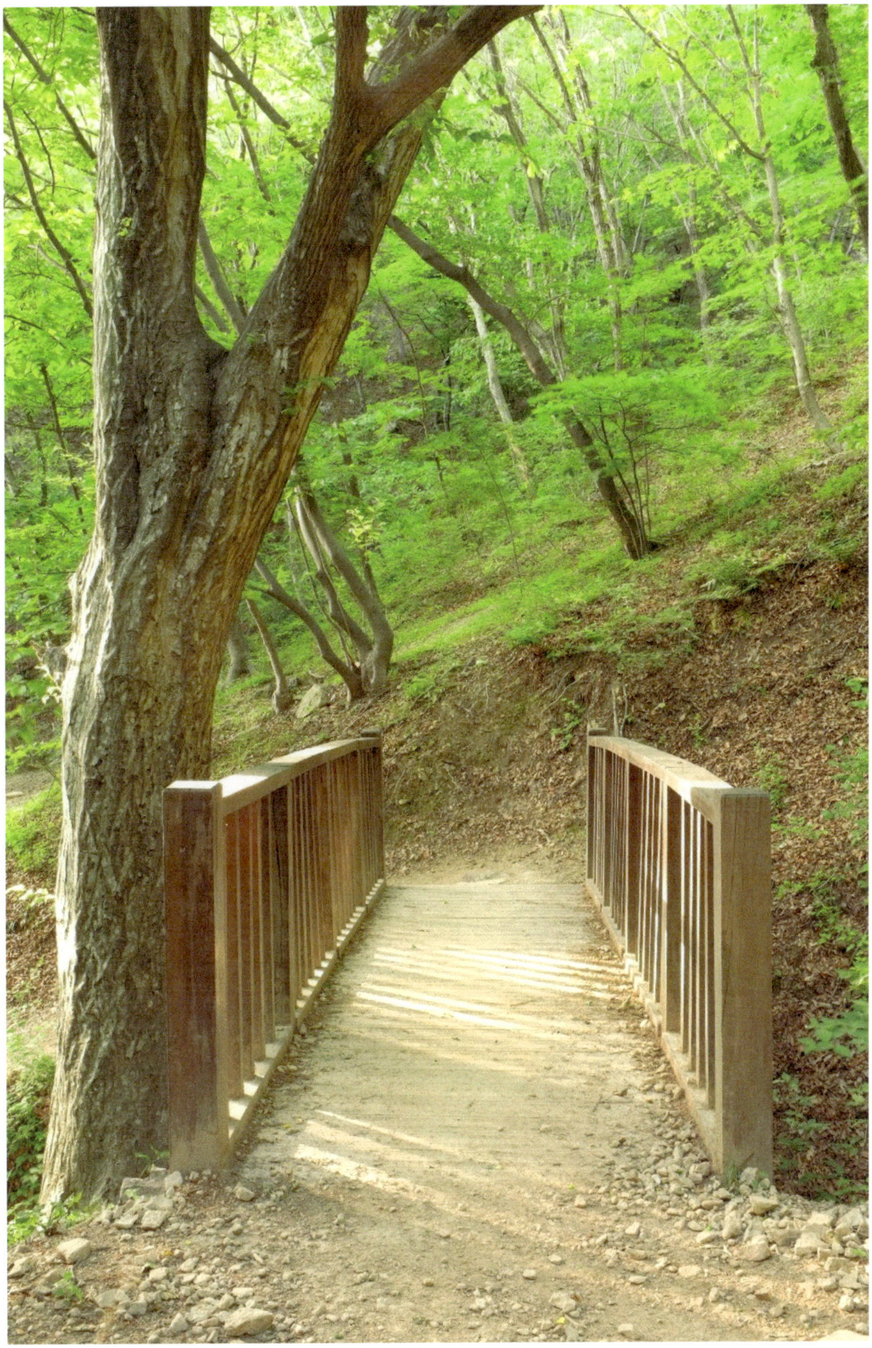

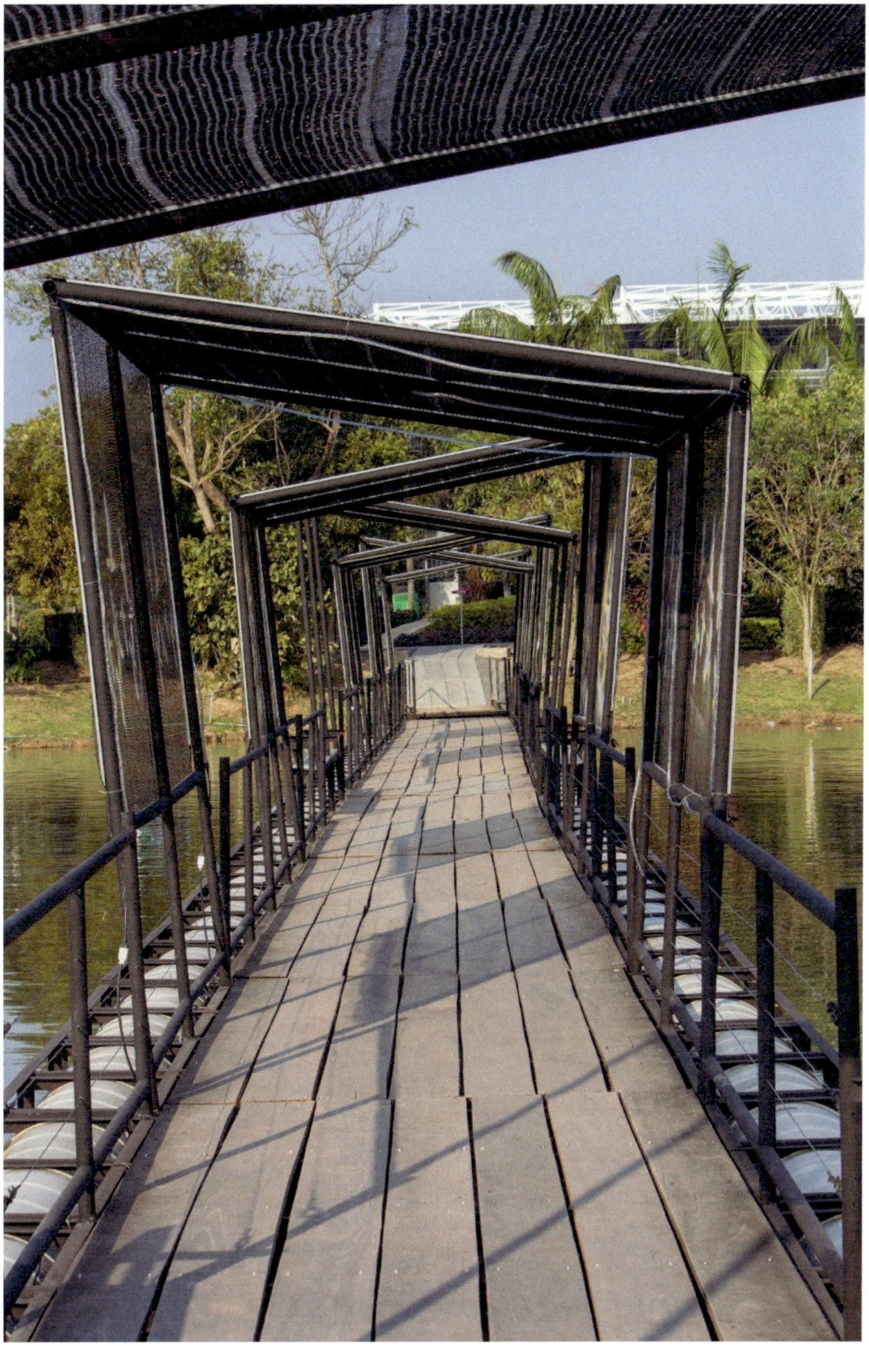

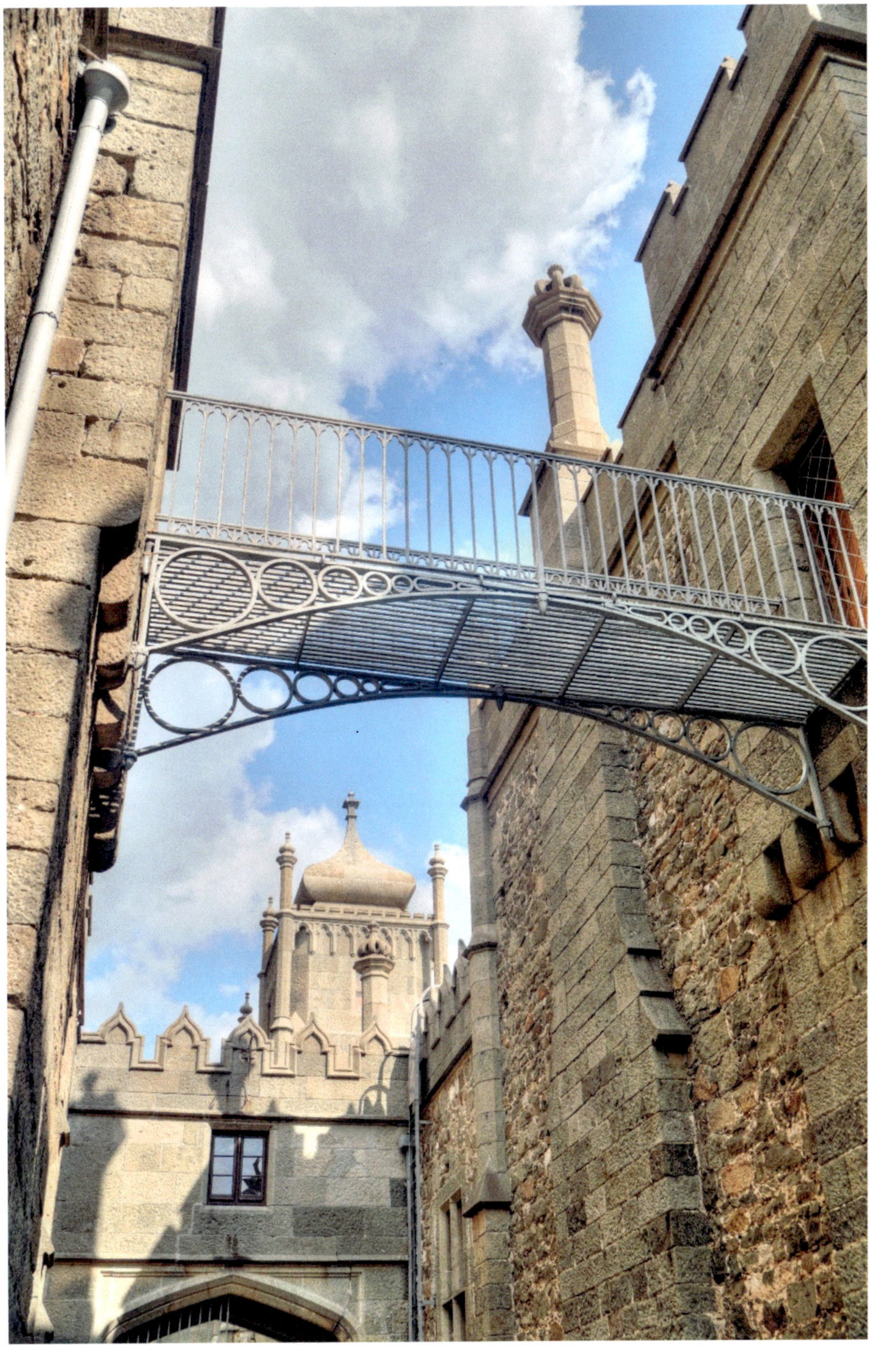

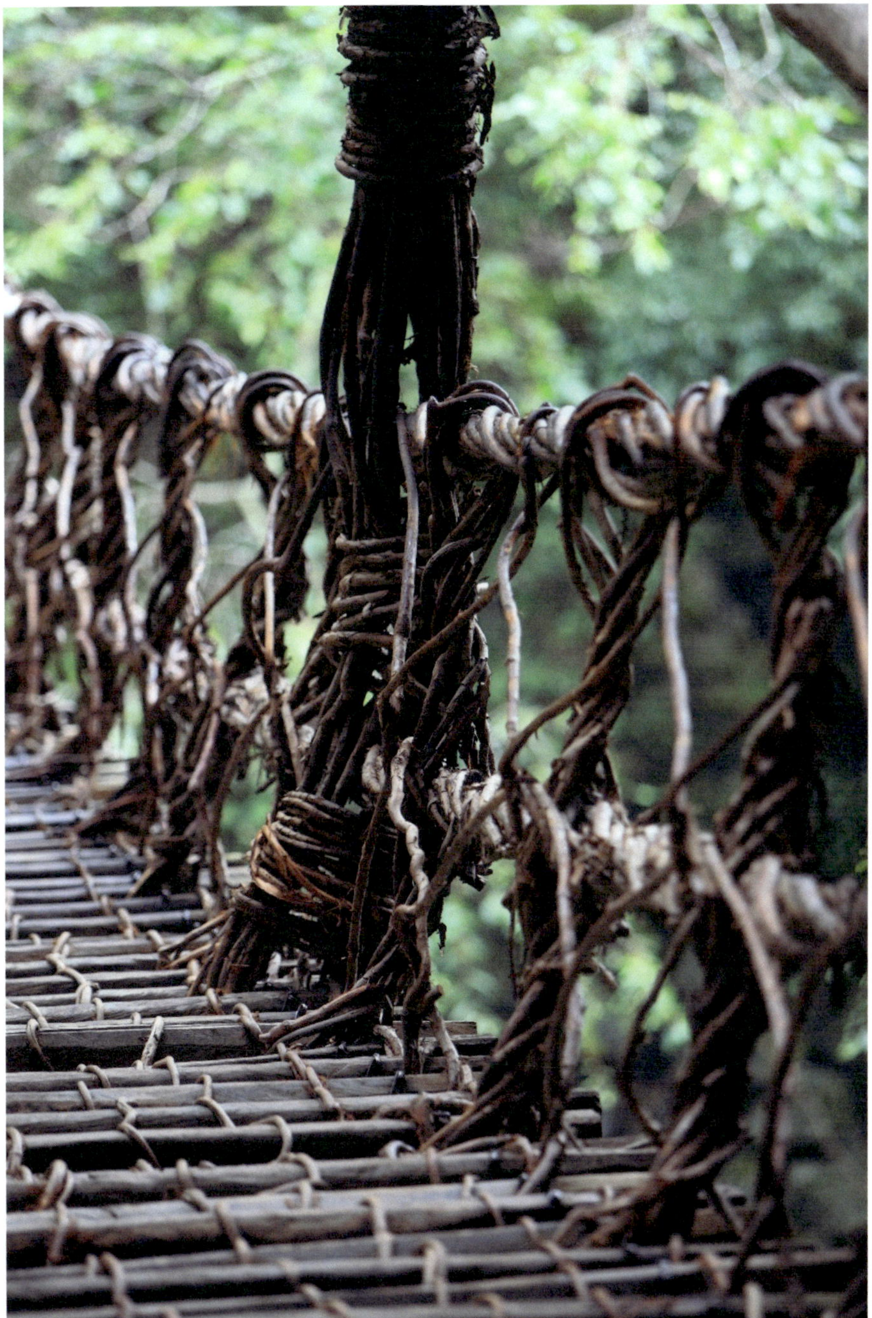

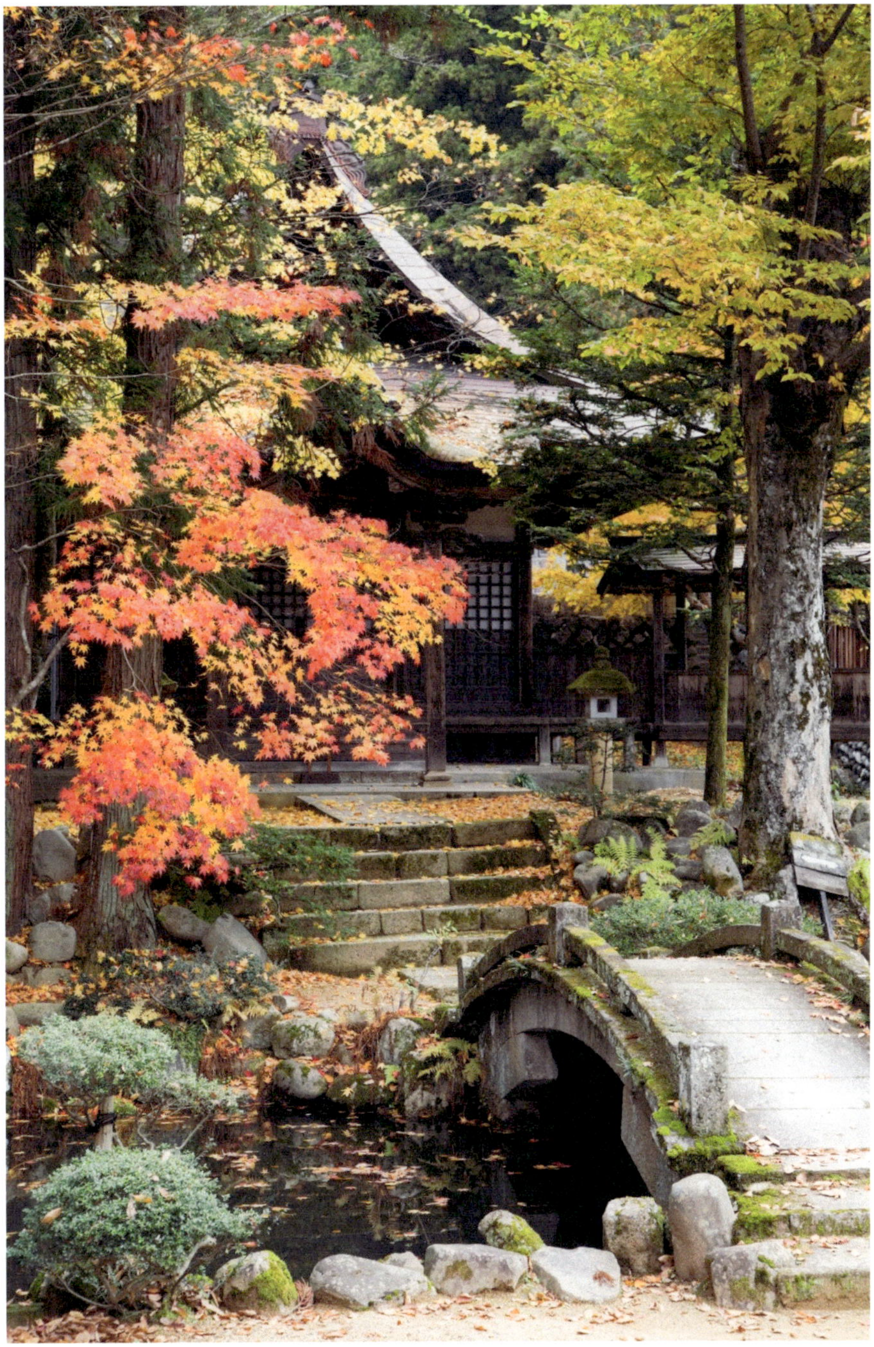

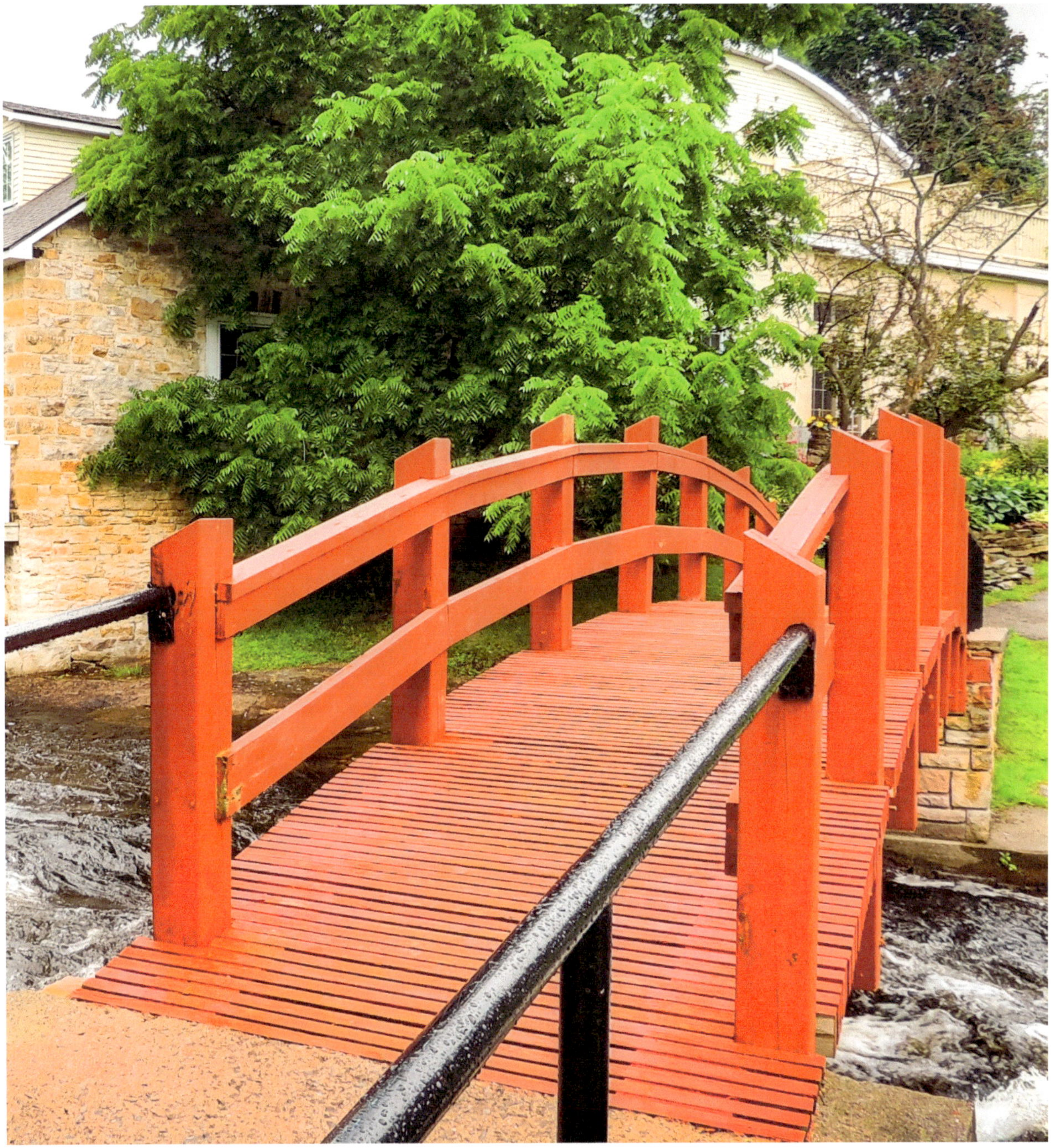

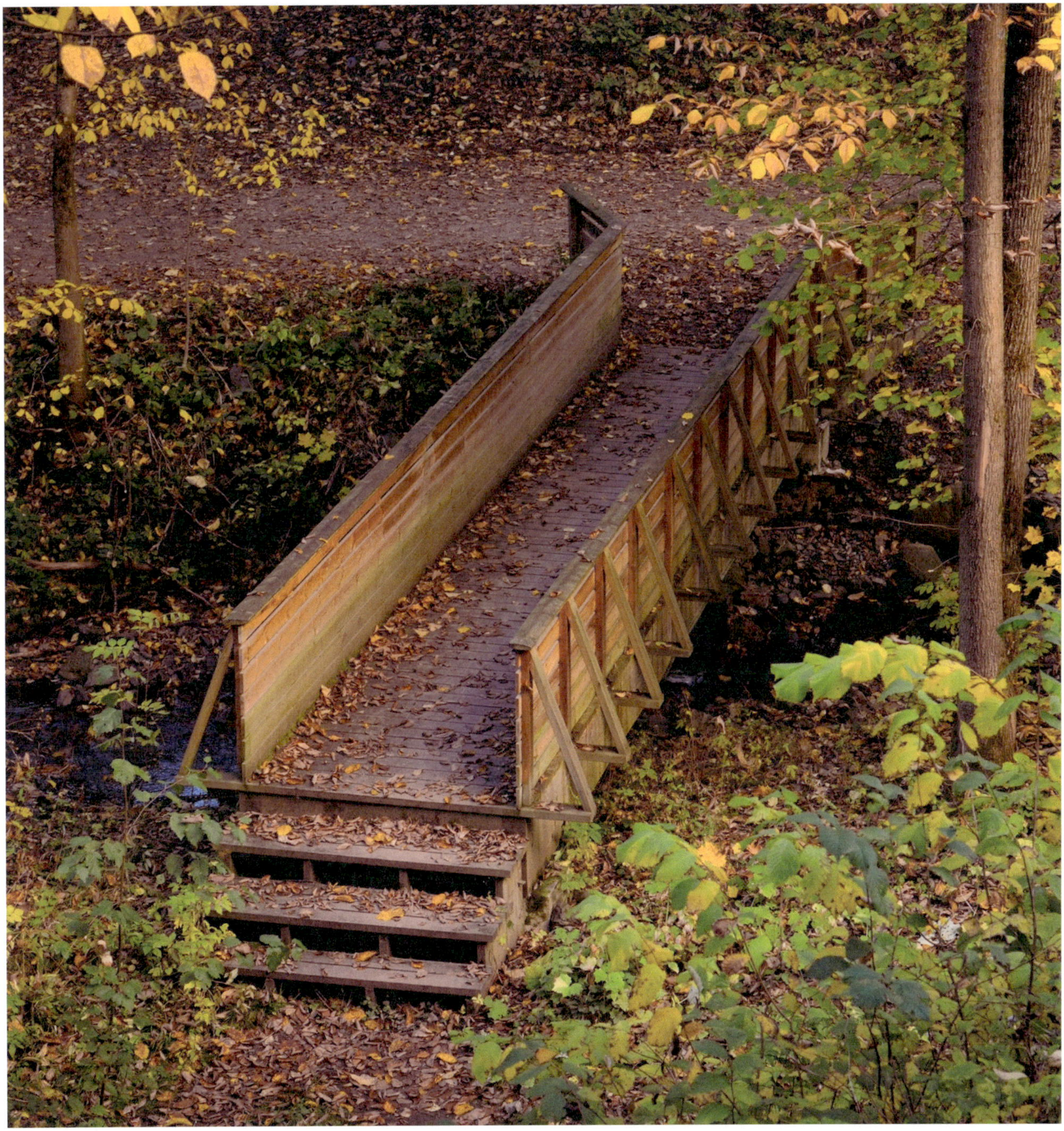

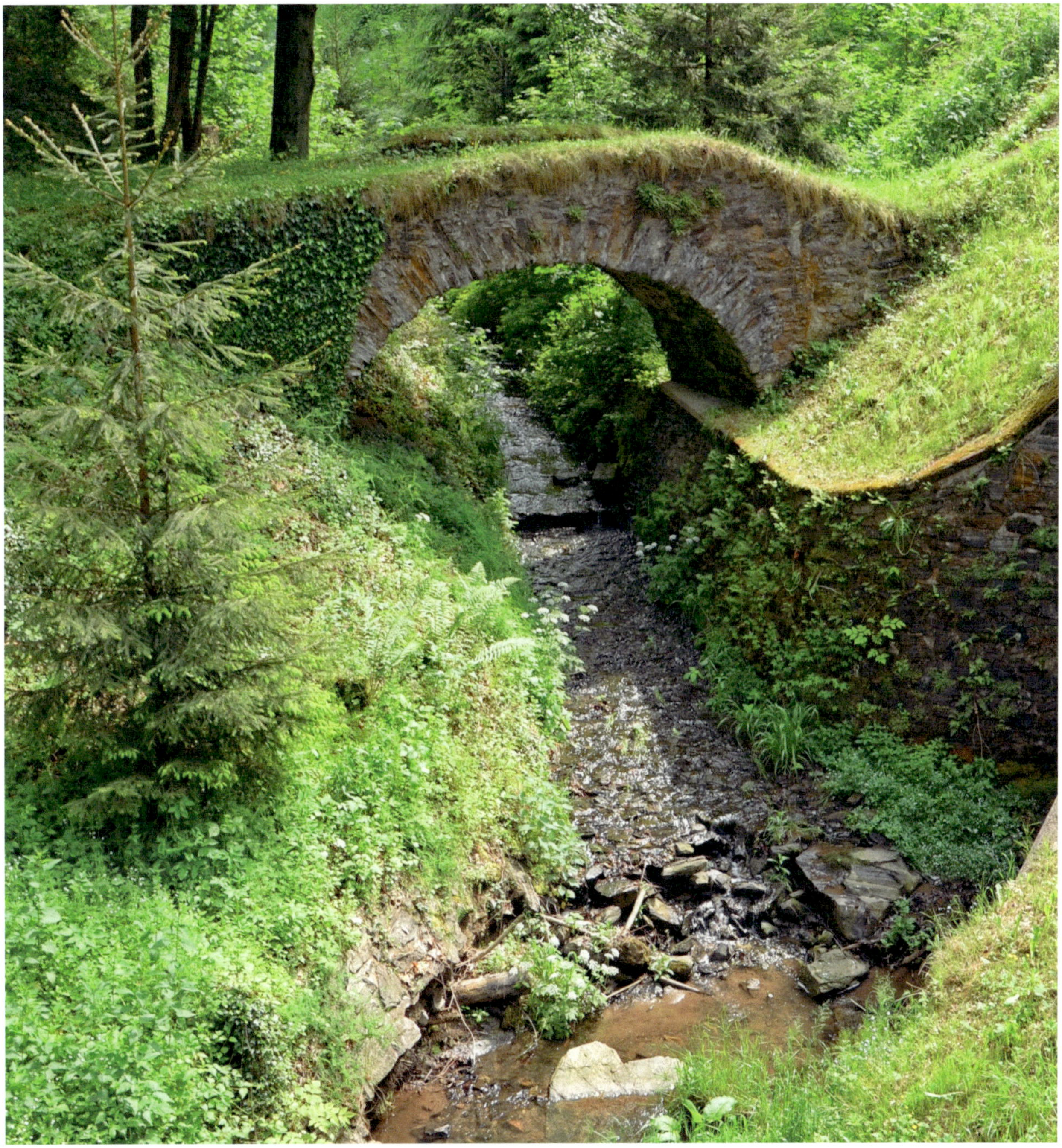

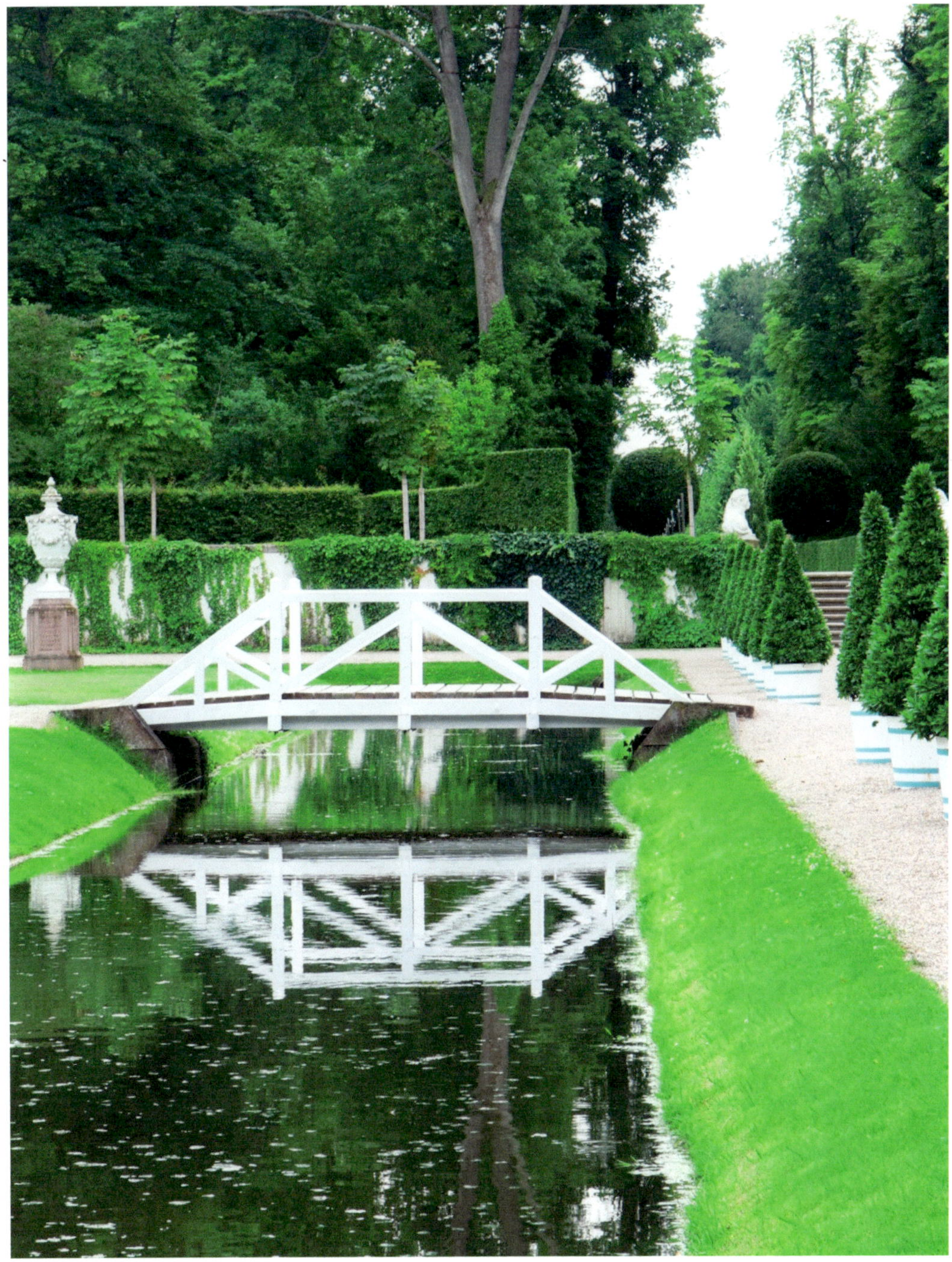

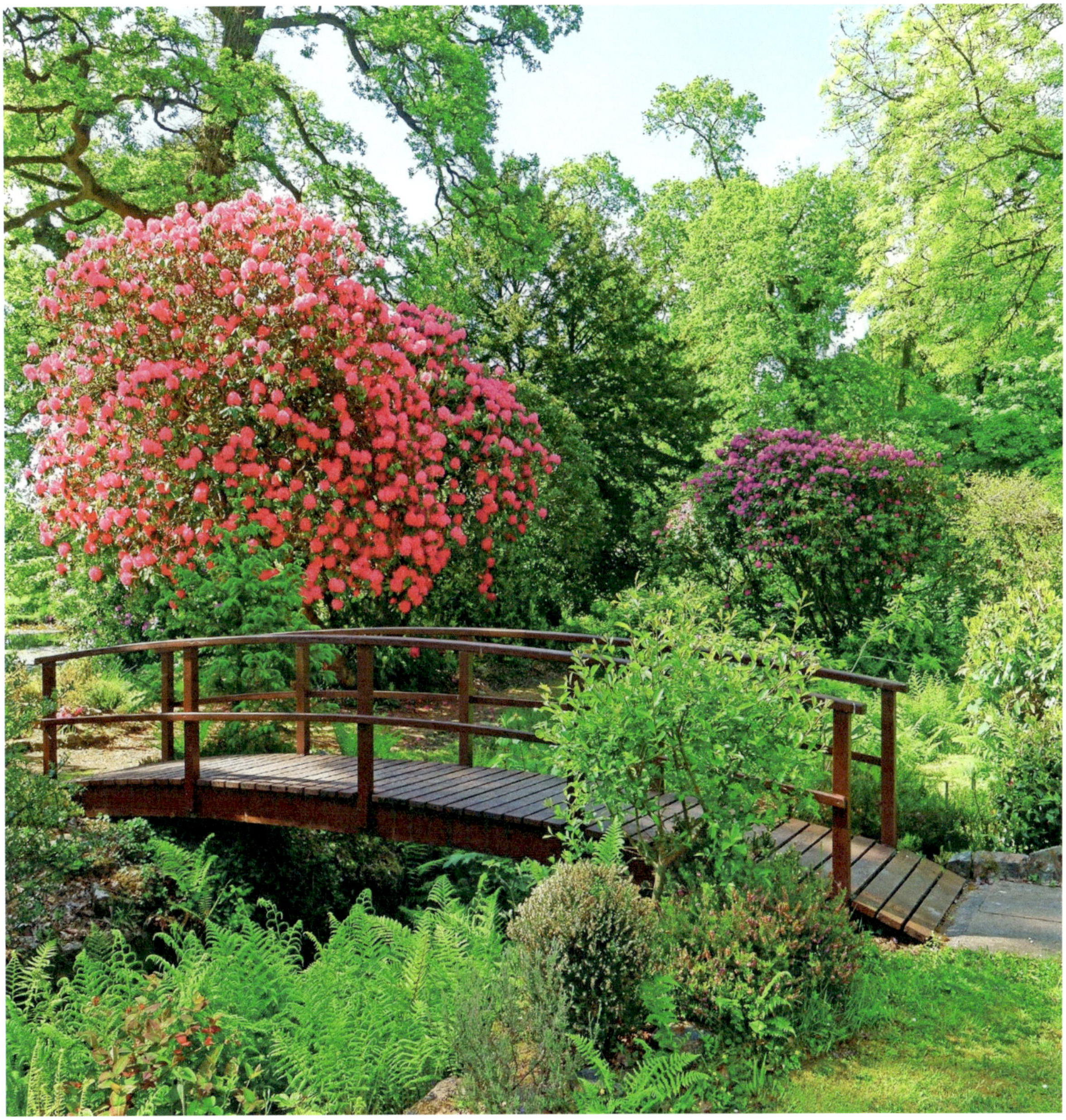

Photo Credits

The artist/source credits for the photos in this book are listed in the order in which they appear:

Cover: Slhy/Shutterstock
InnaFelker/Shutterstock
Anton Mezinov/Shutterstock
LingHK/Shutterstock
Peter Turner Photography/Shutterstock
gorillaimages/Shutterstock
Snvv/Shutterstock
isarescheewin/Shutterstock
Serg64/Shutterstock
Ramon Espelt Photography/Shutterstock
slhy/Shutterstock
Luigi Masella/Shutterstock
Lilly38/Shutterstock
24Novembers/Shutterstock
iravgustin/Shutterstock
MR.TEERASAK KHEMNGERN/Shutterstock
kaman985shu/Shutterstock
alexsvirid/Shutterstock
Pavelk/Shutterstock
Kenneth Keifer/Shutterstock
FooTToo/Shutterstock
robert cicchetti/Shutterstock
TalyaPhoto/Shutterstock
C.K.Ma/Shutterstock
HoleInTheBox/Shutterstock
Kosobu/Shutterstock
Pawel Kazmierczak/Shutterstock
Marques/Shutterstock
Dalibor Sevaljevic/Shutterstock
Brian A Jackson/Shutterstock
Volga/Shutterstock
rsooll/Shutterstock
evantravels/Shutterstock
sanyanwuji/Shutterstock
KPG_Payless/Shutterstock
Boris Puhanic/Shutterstock
bunnyphoto/Shutterstock
rtem/Shutterstock
KPG_Payless/Shutterstock
bikeriderlondon/Shutterstock
alleyboi63/Shutterstock
Marina_89/Shutterstock
bopra77/Shutterstock
AlinaMD/Shutterstock
Peter Raymond Llewellyn/Shutterstock

Made in the USA
Columbia, SC
31 December 2023